People

Parents

by Jennifer L. Marks

Consulting Editor: Gail Saunders-Smith, PhD

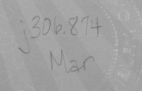

Capstone
press.

Mankato, Minnesota

Pebble Books are published by Capstone Press,
151 Good Counsel Drive, P.O. Box 669, Mankato, Minnesota 56002.
www.capstonepress.com

1 2 3 4 5 6 14 13 12 11 10 09

Library of Congress Cataloging-in-Publication Data
Marks, Jennifer, 1979–
    Parents / by Jennifer L. Marks. — Rev. and updated ed.
    p. cm. — (Pebble books. People)
    Includes bibliographical references and index.
    Summary: "In simple text and photos, presents parents and activities
they do" — Provided by publisher.
    ISBN-13: 978-1-4296-2240-0 (hardcover)
    ISBN-10: 1-4296-2240-7 (hardcover)
    ISBN-13: 978-1-4296-3463-2 (softcover)
    ISBN-10: 1-4296-3463-4 (softcover)
    1. Parent and child — Juvenile literature. 2. Parents — Juvenile literature.
I. Title.
HQ755.85.M266 2009
306.874 — dc22   2008026953

Note to Parents and Teachers

The People set supports national social studies standards related
to individual development and identity. This book describes
and illustrates parents. The images support early readers in
understanding the text. The repetition of words and phrases helps
early readers learn new words. This book also introduces early
readers to subject-specific vocabulary words, which are defined
in the Glossary section. Early readers may need assistance to read
some words and to use the Table of Contents, Glossary, Read More,
Internet Sites, and Index sections of the book.

Table of Contents

What Are Parents?

Parents are people
who raise children.
Mothers and fathers
are parents.

Parents love, protect, teach, and play with their children.

Fathers

Fathers listen.

Matt tells his father

about baseball practice.

Fathers help.
Katie's father
helps her with homework
after school.

Fathers teach.

Mike's father teaches
him about flowers.

14

Mothers

Mothers protect.
Lexi's mother checks
her helmet before
she skateboards.

Mothers help.
Kyle and his mother
bake pizzas
on Saturday.

Mothers play.
Brenna and her mother
shoot hoops.

A Family

Together, children
and parents are a family.

Glossary

family — a group of people related to one another

father — a male parent

mother — a female parent

parent — a mother or a father of one child or many children

practice — to repeat an action over and over in order to improve a skill

protect — to keep someone or something safe

Read More

Easterling, Lisa. *Families.* Our Global Community. Chicago: Marshall Cavendish Benchmark, 2007.

Schaefer, Lola M. *Fathers.* Families. Mankato, Minn.: Capstone Press, 2008.

Schaefer, Lola M. *Mothers.* Families. Mankato, Minn.: Capstone Press, 2008.

Internet Sites

FactHound offers a safe, fun way to find educator-approved Internet sites related to this book.

Here's what you do:
1. Visit *www.facthound.com*
2. Choose your grade level.
3. Begin your search.

This book's ID number is 9781429622400.

FactHound will fetch the best sites for you!

Index

Word Count: 82
Grade: 1
Early-Intervention Level: 12

Credits
Sarah L. Schuette, editor; Abbey Fitzgerald, designer; Marcy Morin, photo
    shoot scheduler

Photo Credits
Capstone Press/Karon Dubke, all

The author dedicates this book to her parents, Leonard Marks,
    and Marlene and Dave Gulden.